The Wild World of Animals

Chimpanzees

Living in Communities

by Erika L. Shores

Consultant:
Patti Ragan
Director
Center for Great Apes
Wauchula, Florida

Bridgestone Books
an imprint of Capstone Press
Mankato, Minnesota

Capstone Press
151 Good Counsel Drive, P.O. Box 669, Mankato, Minnesota 56002
www.capstonepress.com

Library of Congress Cataloging-in-Publication Data
Shores, Erika L., 1976–
    Chimpanzees: living in communities / by Erika L. Shores.
    p. cm.—(The wild world of animals)
    Includes bibliographical references (p. 24) and index.
    ISBN 0-7368-2613-0 (hardcover)
    1. Chimpanzees—Juvenile literature. [1. Chimpanzees.] I. Title. II. Series.
QL737.P96S48 2005
599.885—dc22   2003024648

Summary: An introduction to chimpanzees describing their physical characteristics, habitat, young, food, predators, and relationship to people.

Editorial Credits
Amanda Doering, editor; Linda Clavel, designer; Scott Thoms, photo researcher;
    Eric Kudalis, product planning editor

Photo Credits
Corbis/Karl Ammann, 20; Randy Wells, 14; Tom Brakefield, 18
Creatas, cover
Digital Vision, 1, 8
Ernest H. Rogers, 6
GeoIMAGERY, 12
McDonald Wildlife Photography/Joe McDonald, 10
Nature Picture Library, 4
Tom Stack & Associates/Mark Newman, 16

Table of Contents

arms

head

legs

feet

Chimpanzees

Chimpanzees stand about 4 feet (1.2 meters) tall. They weigh 60 to 120 pounds (27 to 54 kilograms). Chimpanzees' arms are longer than their legs. Black hair covers most of a chimpanzee's body.

Chimpanzees usually walk on their hands and feet. Chimpanzees also can stand and walk upright.

Chimpanzees Are Mammals

Chimpanzees are **mammals**. They are warm-blooded. Female chimpanzees feed milk to their young. Chimpanzees belong to a group of mammals called **primates**. People also are primates.

warm-blooded

having a body temperature that stays the same

Where Chimpanzees Live

Chimpanzees live in Africa. Their habitats include rain forests, **savannas**, and woodlands. Chimpanzees sleep in trees. They use leaves and branches to make nests. Chimpanzees sleep safely in their nests.

habitat
the place and natural conditions in which an animal lives

10

Chimpanzees live together in **communities**. These groups include up to 120 chimpanzees. Chimpanzees use sounds and touch to communicate with each other. Certain sounds warn chimpanzees of danger. Chimpanzees touch to show feelings.

communicate
to share information, ideas, or feelings

FUN FACTS

Chimpanzees also make rocks into tools. They use rocks as hammers to break open nutshells.

What Chimpanzees Eat

Chimpanzees eat fruit, nuts, seeds, and insects. They are **omnivores**. Chimpanzees use tools to help them get food. They poke sticks into ant or termite nests. The insects crawl onto the stick. Chimpanzees then eat the insects off the sticks.

Mating and Birth

Male and female chimpanzees mate. Female chimpanzees give birth eight months later. Young chimpanzees are called infants. Chimpanzees usually have only one infant. Female chimpanzees can give birth every five to six years.

mate
to join together to produce young

Chimpanzee Infants

Newborn infants are small and helpless. They weigh 3 pounds (1.4 kilograms) at birth. Mothers carry their infants wherever they go. An infant hangs onto its mother's stomach or rides on her back.

Chimpanzees can live to be 50 years old.

18

Predators

Leopards, cheetahs, and some snakes hunt chimpanzees. Chimpanzees have ways to stay safe from **predators**. They make loud warning calls when predators are near. They also may throw rocks and sticks at predators.

FUN FACTS

Jane Goodall is a famous scientist. She has studied chimpanzees for more than 40 years.

Chimpanzees and People

People have helped and harmed chimpanzees. Scientists help people learn about chimpanzees. Other people harm chimpanzees. They cut down forests where chimpanzees live. Today, many people work to protect chimpanzees and their habitats.

scientist

a person who studies the world around us

Hands On: Foot Work

Chimpanzees have fingers and thumbs. They even have thumbs on their feet. Chimpanzees can pick up objects with their hands and feet. Try this game with some friends to see if you can pick up things with your feet.

What You Need

2 friends
3 chairs
3 small sticks
3 oranges
3 bananas
3 shoeboxes of the same size

What You Do

1. Place the chairs next to each other in a row.
2. Place a stick, an orange, a banana, and a shoebox in front of each chair.
3. All three players sit in a chair. The players take off their shoes and socks.
4. Players race to see who can pick up all three objects with their feet and put them in the box first. Players do not have to stay on the chairs.
5. Once all three players have the items in the box, see who can take the items out of the box with their feet the fastest.

Glossary

community (kuh-MYOO-nuh-tee)—a group of animals that live in the same area

mammal (MAM-uhl)—a warm-blooded animal with a backbone and hair or fur; female mammals produce milk to feed their young.

omnivore (OM-nuh-vor)—an animal that eats plants and other animals

predator (PRED-uh-tur)—an animal that hunts other animals for food

primate (PRYE-mate)—any animal in the group of mammals that includes humans, apes, and monkeys

savanna (suh-VAN-uh)—a flat, grassy plain with few or no trees

Read More

Jacobs, Liza. *Chimpanzees.* Wild Wild World. San Diego: Blackbirch Press, 2003.

Kendell, Patricia. *Chimpanzees.* In the Wild. Austin, Texas: Raintree Steck-Vaughn, 2002.

Murray, Julie. *Chimpanzees.* Animal Kingdom. Edina, Minn.: Abdo, 2002.

Internet Sites

FactHound offers a safe, fun way to find Internet sites related to this book. All of the sites on FactHound have been researched by our staff.

Here's how:
1. Visit *www.facthound.com*
2. Type in this special code **0736826130** for age-appropriate sites. Or enter a search word related to this book for a more general search.
3. Click on the **Fetch It** button.

FactHound will fetch the best sites for you!

Index